Jamaica

IMMIGRATION TODAY

Maya Logan

PICTURE CREDITS

Cover: African-American family sitting on a wall, Inmagine.

Page 1 © Ramin Talaie/Corbis/Tranz; page 4 (left) © Ted Spiegel/ Corbis/Tranz; page 4 (right) © 2006 Kayte Deioma; page 5 (top) © Diane Bondareff/AP Photo/AAP; page 5 (bottom) © Stock Central; page 6 © Alain Le Garsmeur/Corbis/Tranz; page 8 © Photolibrary; page 9 © Robert Harding/Robert Harding World Imagery/Getty Images; page 11 © Steve Starr/Corbis/Tranz; pages 12–13 © Stock Central; page 14 © Mario Tama/Getty Images; page 15 © Beth A. Keiser/AP Photo/AAP; page 16 © Ted Spiegel/Corbis/ Tranz; page 22 (top) © Howard Davies/Corbis/Tranz; page 22 (bottom) © Andrew Aguilar; page 23 © Sergio Pitamitz/Corbis/ Tranz; page 24 © Audrius Tomonis/www.banknotes.com; page 25 © Photolibrary; page 26 (top) © Nik Wheeler/Corbis/Tranz; page 26 (bottom) © Dave G. Houser/Post-Houserstock/Corbis/ Tranz; page 29 © David R. Frazier/DanitaDelimont.com.

Produced through the worldwide resources of the National Geographic Society, John M. Fahey, Jr., President and Chief Executive Officer; Gilbert M. Grosvenor, Chairman of the Board.

PREPARED BY NATIONAL GEOGRAPHIC SCHOOL PUBLISHING
Sheron Long, Chief Executive Officer; Samuel Gesumaria, President; Steve Mico, Executive Vice President and Publisher; Francis Downey, Editor in Chief; Richard Easby, Editorial Manager; Margaret Sidlosky, Director of Design and Illustrations; Jim Hiscott, Design Manager; Cynthia Olson and Ruth Ann Thompson, Art Directors; Matt Wascavage, Director of Publishing Services; Lisa Pergolizzi, Production Manager.

MANUFACTURING AND QUALITY CONTROL
Christopher A. Liedel, Chief Financial Officer; Phillip L. Schlosser, Vice President; Clifton M. Brown III, Director.

EDITOR
Mary Anne Wengel

PROGRAM CONSULTANTS
Dr. Shirley V. Dickson, National Literacy Consultant; Margit E. McGuire, Ph.D., Professor of Teacher Education and Social Studies, Seattle University.

National Geographic Theme Sets program developed by Macmillan Education Australia Pty Limited.

Published by the National Geographic Society
1145 17th Street, N.W.
Washington, D.C. 20036-4688

ISBN: 978-1-4263-5179-2

Printed in China

13 14 15 16 17 18 19 20 21
10 9 8 7 6 5 4 3

Contents

Immigration to the United States

Immigrants are people who leave their own country to go and live in another country. People have been immigrating to the United States for hundreds of years. New immigrants arrive each year. They make the United States their home. Today, many Americans can trace their roots back to another country. Ukraine, Guatemala, Jamaica, and Vietnam are some of the countries new immigrants come from.

Key Concepts

1. People choose to immigrate for many different reasons.
2. People who immigrate face many challenges.
3. People who immigrate contribute to the life and culture of the United States.

Four Groups of Immigrants

Ukrainian

Ukrainian immigrants come from Ukraine in Europe.

Guatemalan

Guatemalan immigrants come from Guatemala in Central America.

In this book you will learn about people who immigrate from Jamaica.

Jamaican

Jamaican immigrants come from Jamaica in the Caribbean.

Vietnamese

Vietnamese immigrants come from Vietnam in Asia.

Immigration from Jamaica

Imagine you live in a country that is poor. It is hard to find a job. There are very few opportunities. Many people around you are poor and jobless. Would you leave your country to look for a better life in a new place? Many people from Jamaica leave their country to come to the United States. They come in search of a better life and more opportunities.

Jamaica

Jamaica is an island. It is part of an island group called the West Indies. Jamaica is located in the Caribbean Sea. It is about the size of Connecticut. Jamaica used to be ruled by Britain. The people there speak mainly English.

People in the city of Kingston, Jamaica

Britain ruled Jamaica for 300 years. In 1962, Jamaica became independent. More than 90 percent of Jamaicans are descendants of people who came from Africa. They were brought to Jamaica as slaves hundreds of years ago.

Many people from Jamaica have come to live in the United States. More people continue to arrive each year.

The map below shows where Jamaica is located in the West Indies.

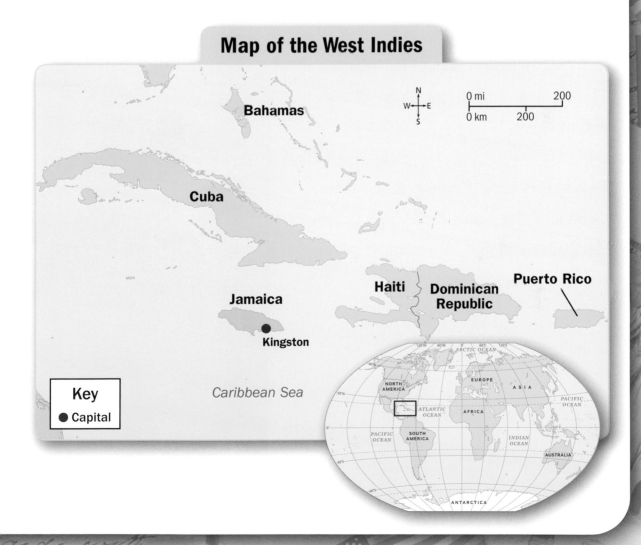

Map of the West Indies

Bahamas

Cuba

Haiti

Dominican Republic

Puerto Rico

Jamaica

Kingston

Caribbean Sea

Key
● Capital

Why People Immigrate

People who leave their country to go and live in another country are called immigrants. People **immigrate** for many reasons. These reasons are called "push factors" and "pull factors."

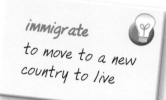

immigrate
to move to a new
country to live

Push factors encourage people to leave a place. They make life hard. **Poverty** and **unemployment** are push factors. War, crime, and bad weather can all be push factors. Hurricanes often hit Jamaica. These big storms can wreck buildings and hurt people.

Pull factors draw people to a new place. Good jobs and a safe life are pull factors. Both push and pull factors cause people to immigrate.

A Jamaican man digs out a car buried by a hurricane.

Leaving Jamaica Over the years, many factors have pushed Jamaicans to immigrate. In the 1970s, violence was the main push factor. Thousands of Jamaicans moved to the United States to escape violence. The violence took place between political groups. Each group wanted their political party to govern Jamaica. The island became a dangerous place to live. People wanted to escape from the violence.

Today, poverty pushes people to immigrate. Jamaica has a weak **economy.** This means that many people are poor. Many people do not have jobs. Many people cannot afford good housing. It is hard to get good health care. It is hard to find the money to go to college. Many people leave Jamaica in search of a better life.

Poor people in Jamaica live in houses such as these.

Coming to the United States Many Jamaicans are pulled to the United States. The United States is a rich country. It has a stable economy. It has strict laws that make people feel safe and secure. There are jobs here. People in the United States can earn good wages. There are good schools and colleges here. Many people enjoy a high standard of living in the United States.

Some people from Jamaica come to join family members who have already settled in the United States.

The bar graph below shows you how many Jamaicans immigrated to the United States between 1951 and 2000.

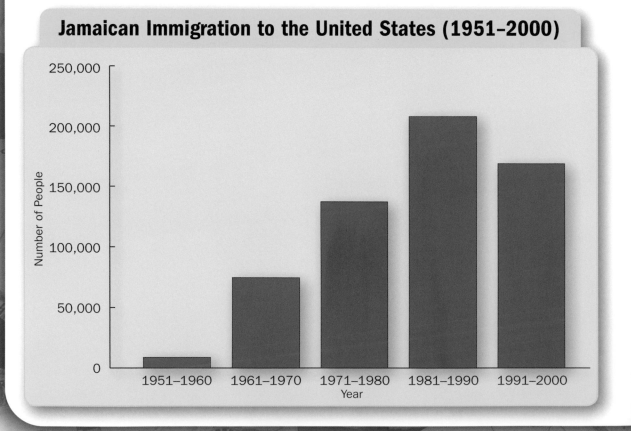

Jamaican Immigration to the United States (1951–2000)

The Challenges of Immigration

Jamaican immigrants face many **challenges.**
They have to get used to many new things.
They must find new homes and jobs.

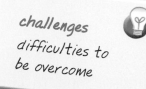

challenges
difficulties to
be overcome

Many people in Jamaica are poor. People who want to move must save the money to make the trip. This can take a long time.

A big challenge for Jamaican immigrants is finding a job. Sometimes, new immigrants find jobs they like. At other times, they have to take any job they can find. They have to earn money to support themselves.

Many immigrants leave their families behind. They miss their families. Many Jamaicans come to the United States to earn money to send back to Jamaica. They come prepared to work hard.

This Jamaican man works hard at a sugarcane farm in the United States.

Learning New Ways Coming to a new country means having to learn new ways. Unlike immigrants from some countries, Jamaicans speak English. Being able to write and speak English makes it easier for them to find jobs. It makes it easier to carry out daily tasks.

There are things Jamaican immigrants have to get used to. One of these things is food. In Jamaica, people eat a lot of fruits and vegetables. They like bananas, breadfruit, and yams. Jamaicans also like to eat pork, chicken, and goat meat. They make spicy dishes with meat and vegetables.

In the United States, Jamaicans have to change their diets. People eat more meat in the United States. Fruits cost more here than in Jamaica. Immigrants have to change what they buy and how they cook their food.

Jamaicans eat a mixture of traditional Jamaican food and American food.

Fitting into American Life Fitting into American life is not easy for new immigrants. **Discrimination** is one problem some immigrants face. Many Jamaicans who come to the United States are skilled and well educated. Yet they are sometimes treated unfairly because they are from a different place. Employers may refuse to give them jobs. Or they may give them jobs with low pay. Discrimination is against the law, yet it still occurs.

Jamaican children also face challenges. They may feel lonely at first. They speak with a different accent, and are from a different **culture.** In time, they overcome their fears, make new friends, and settle in.

Children from different cultural backgrounds learn together in American schools.

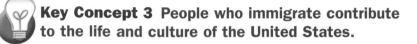

Joining American Society

Jamaican-Americans are part of American society. They **contribute** to society in many ways. They bring their skills and experiences to the United States. They work in supermarkets, hospitals, and hotels. Many Jamaicans own restaurants and stores. They sell Jamaican food, clothes, and music.

contribute
to give toward a
common purpose

Like all Americans, immigrants contribute to the economy. They do this by paying **taxes.** The government uses this money to provide things people need. Taxes help pay for roads, public transport, schools, and hospitals.

Jamaican immigrants also bring their culture with them. They share their culture with people in their new country. All people in the United States then get to enjoy Jamaican culture.

This man is cooking Jamaican chicken for people at Mardi Gras in New Orleans.

Keeping Jamaican Culture Alive

Jamaican-Americans keep their culture alive. They do this by celebrating and sharing their traditions. One tradition they share is their love of **carnivals.**

Carnival is now a big event in the United States. The first celebration takes place in Atlanta on Memorial Day weekend. Over the next five months, events are held in other cities. The largest Carnival takes place in Brooklyn, New York, on Labor Day. Almost three million people join the street parades. They wear colorful masks, sing, and dance.

This man is wearing a colorful costume at Carnival in New York.

Jamaican food, dance, and art have become popular in the United States. Jamaican music, such as soca, calypso, and **reggae,** is now popular. Jamaican music is played at street parades and carnivals held to celebrate Jamaican culture.

Many Jamaican immigrants have built their own churches in the United States. Church is an important part of life for many Jamaicans. They like to worship in the same way people in Jamaica do. It helps them remember the country they left. It helps keep their culture alive.

Jamaican women play steel drums in Brooklyn, New York City.

Think About the **Key Concepts**

Think about what you read. Think about the pictures and diagrams. Use these to answer the questions. Share what you think with others.

1. What pushes people to immigrate to the United States? What pulls them?

2. What challenges do immigrants face to get to a new country?

3. What do immigrants have to do to fit into a new country?

4. How does the immigrant group in this book keep their culture alive?

Bar Graph

Bar graphs are used to compare different amounts.

A bar graph uses bars to show amounts being compared. Look back at the bar graph on page 10. It shows the number of Jamaican immigrants who came to the United States from 1951 to 2000. Each bar shows the number of people who immigrated that year.

The graph on page 19 is also a bar graph. It shows the number of immigrants from four countries in 2004. The bar graph allows you to compare the number of people in each group.

How to Read a Bar Graph

1. Read the title.
   The title tells you what information the bar graph shows.

2. Read the key.
   The key tells you what information is being compared.

3. Get the general idea.
   On the bar graph, the taller bars represent a greater quantity than the shorter bars.

4. Get the details.
   Look at the numbers on the vertical line, or axis. Match that number with the top of each bar. These numbers help you figure out the quantity each bar represents.

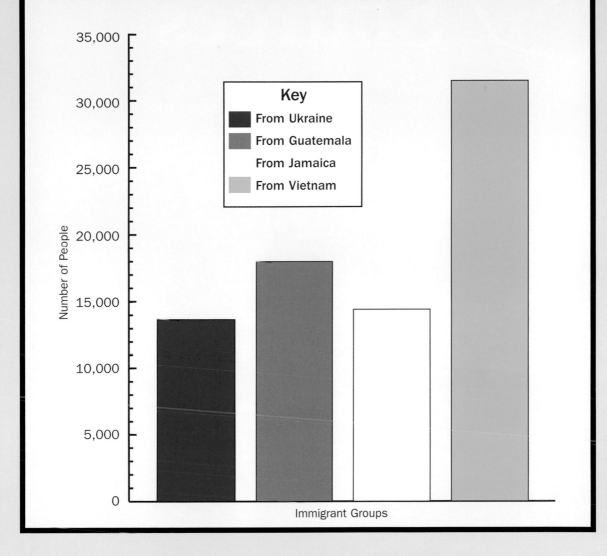

Immigration to the United States (2004)

Number of People — *Immigrant Groups*

Key
- From Ukraine
- From Guatemala
- From Jamaica
- From Vietnam

What Does the Graph Show?

Read the bar graph above. How many people arrived in the United States from each country in 2004? Which group had the largest number of immigrants? Which group had the smallest number? Tell a classmate what you learned from this bar graph.

Reference Sources

The purpose of **reference sources** is to inform. Reference sources can take many forms.

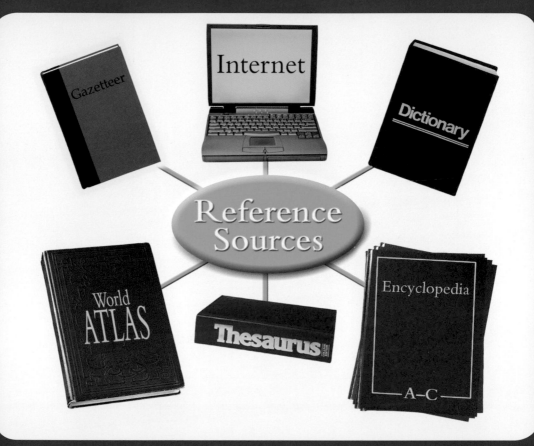

You use different reference sources for different things. For example, if you want to know how to spell *immigration,* use a dictionary. But if you want to know geographical facts about a country, use a **gazetteer.**

You do not read a reference source from beginning to end. You read only the parts that cover topics you want to learn about.

Jamaica
GAZETTEER

The **title** tells you which country the gazetteer is about.

The amount of land a country covers

● Area

Headings name topics.

Jamaica is 4,244 square miles (10,991 square kilometers), an area slightly smaller than the state of Connecticut.

Text gives information about the topic.

● Location

Jamaica is located in the Caribbean Sea. It is one of the islands of the West Indies. The West Indies includes islands such as Cuba, Haiti, and Dominican Republic. Jamaica lies south of Florida.

Maps, photographs, or **diagrams** support the text.

Where a country is in the world and what is around it

Map of Jamaica

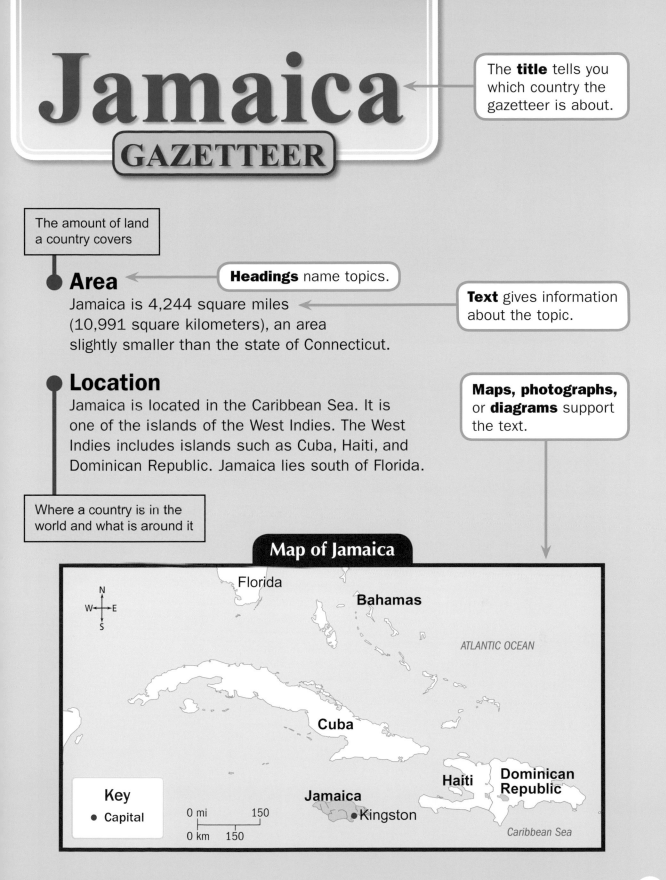

Florida

Bahamas

N
W←┼→E
S

ATLANTIC OCEAN

Cuba

Haiti

Dominican Republic

Key
● Capital

Jamaica
● Kingston

0 mi 150
0 km 150

Caribbean Sea

Capital

The capital of Jamaica is Kingston.

> The city where a country's government has its main office

The business district in downtown Kingston

Major Cities and Towns

Major cities and towns in Jamaica are
- Kingston
- Montego Bay
- Portmore
- Spanish Town

Flag

The Jamaican flag has three colors. The colors are green, black, and gold. Black stands for the hardships people overcome. Gold stands for the sun. Green stands for hope.

Population

The population of Jamaica is 2,758,124 (2006).

> The total number of people in an area

Natural Features

> The physical geography of a country

Nearly half of Jamaica is covered in mountains. There are tall cliffs that drop 984 feet (300 meters) straight down to the ocean.

Along parts of the coast are narrow plains and beaches. The northern coast has white sand beaches. The southern coast has coastal plains and black sand beaches.

The island has different ecosystems. There are forests in the mountains, rain forests in the valleys, grassy plains, and dry, sandy areas.

Jamaica has many beautiful waterfalls and lush vegetation.

Climate

The northeast of Jamaica receives a lot of rain. The southwest receives less rain as the mountains block out winds that carry rain.

The lowlands are warm, with a year round temperature of about 86° Fahrenheit (30° Celsius). The highlands are cooler. The temperature here is always between 59°–71.6° Fahrenheit (15°–22° Celsius).

The bar graph below shows the average rainfall and temperature in the capital, Kingston, which is located in the southeast of the country.

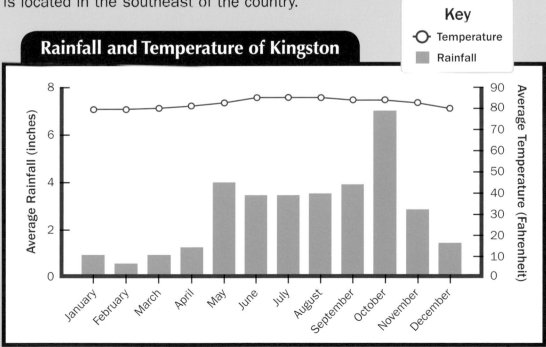

Key
- ⭕ Temperature
- ▮ Rainfall

Rainfall and Temperature of Kingston

Industry

Jamaica has many resources. These include bauxite, aluminum, and metal deposits. It has industries that make clothing, rum, cement, paper, and chemical products. Telecommunications and tourism are important industries in Jamaica as well.

Agriculture

Farm products the country produces

Many crops are grown in Jamaica such as sugarcane, bananas, coffee, cocoa, and citrus fruits. Jamaican coffee from the Blue Mountains is famous all over the world.

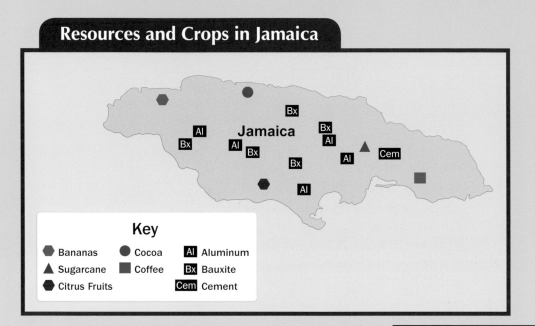

Resources and Crops in Jamaica

Key

- ⬣ Bananas
- ▲ Sugarcane
- ⬡ Citrus Fruits
- ● Cocoa
- ■ Coffee
- Al Aluminum
- Bx Bauxite
- Cem Cement

Exports

Goods a country sells to other countries

Jamaica sells bauxite, aluminum, clothing, sugar, bananas, coffee, citrus, rum, and cocoa to other countries.

Currency

The name of the money people use in a country

The currency of Jamaica is the Jamaican dollar (JMD).

A 50 Dollar Jamaican note

Jamaican Celebrations

Jamaicans celebrate many religious festivals. Independence Day is also important to Jamaicans. Jamaicans have several carnivals a year. These are colorful, with a lot of music.

New Year's Day
Jamaicans visit friends between Christmas and New Year's Day.

Carnival
February is carnival month in Jamaica. People celebrate with parades, music, and dancing.

Emancipation Day
People celebrate the end of 400 years of Jamaican slavery.

National Heroes Day
Jamaicans remember their national heroes.

January

February

March

April

May

June

July

August

September

October

November

December

Easter
A week-long Jamaican Carnival begins on Easter Day.

Labor Day
Jamaicans do community service. They fix roads, paint schools, and plant trees.

Independence Day
Jamaicans celebrate the day they received independence. People make floats for parades and dance in the street.

Christmas
Christmas is a big family event. Jamaicans go to church, exchange gifts, and have a feast.

Religion

Most of the people in Jamaica are Christians.
About 60 percent of them are Protestants.
About 10 percent are Catholics.

Food

Jamaican cooking is based on African,
European, Asian, and Middle Eastern food.

Some popular Jamaican dishes are
- jerk (meat rubbed with spices)
- grilled meat
- smoked fish
- spicy seafood dishes
- saltfish and ackee (a type of fruit)
- fried plantains (large bananas)
- rice and peas

Only the fleshy part around the
seed of the ackee can be eaten.

Cutting jerk chicken
with a cleaver

Languages

English and Jamaican Creole are widely spoken
in Jamaica.

Apply the **Key Concepts**

Key Concept 1 People choose to immigrate for many different reasons.

Activity Create a concept web. Write down the things that make people decide to immigrate. Include reasons that push people to move from Jamaica. Also include reasons that pull people to the United States.

No Jobs

Reason to Immigrate

Key Concept 2 People who immigrate face many challenges.

Activity Make a list of the challenges new immigrants may face when they move to the United States. If you were a new immigrant, how would you overcome these challenges? Create an action plan of things you would do to settle and fit into a new country.

Action Plan
1. Take English lessons
2.
3.

Key Concept 3 People who immigrate contribute to the life and culture of the United States.

Activity Create a poster for a Jamaican festival. Think about the things that you would enjoy at a festival. Put them on your poster. For example, what food would you bring? What music would you have? Show the festival attractions on the poster.

JAMAICAN FESTIVAL

Attractions:
•
•

Create Your Own Gazetteer

You have read the gazetteer on Jamaica. Now you can research another country and write a gazetteer for it.

1. Study the Model

Look back at pages 21–26. Think about the type of information a gazetteer contains. How is the gazetteer entry organized? What kinds of headings were used to break the information into easy-to-find sections? What kinds of facts are included about Jamaica? These are the kinds of facts you should include in your gazetteer.

2. Choose a Country

Choose a country you are interested in and would like to know more about. You will now write a gazetteer on that country. Think about the kind of information a reader might look for when using your gazetteer for research. What would a researcher be interested in? This is the type of information you should include in your gazetteer.

Gazetteer Entries

◆ Each entry is about one country.

◆ The title tells us which country the entry is about.

◆ A map helps us locate the country.

◆ The facts tell us important information about the country.

◆ Pictures support the facts and add interest.

3. Research the Topic

Make a list of the kinds of information you will need to find. Use the library or Internet to find the facts and figures you need. Write down all the information that you can use. Look for a map of the country. Look for pictures to include in your gazetteer that support the information you have collected.

Topic: Cuba

1. Where is Cuba located?

2. How many people live there?

3. What are the natural features of the country?

4. Write a Draft

Plan how you are going to organize your gazetteer. Start with a title. The title should name the country you are writing about. Create headings for the different kinds of information you are including. Arrange your headings in the order you would like them to appear. Fit the information you have found under the headings. If you have all the information you need, you can begin writing your gazetteer. If you included pictures, write captions for them.

5. Revise and Edit

Read your draft. Is it easy to quickly see the kinds of information the gazetteer contains? Are all the facts and figures in the gazetteer correct? Look for words that are misspelled. If there are any mistakes, fix them.

Present Your Own Gazetteer

Now you can share your work. Get together with your classmates and put all of your gazetteer entries together into a class gazetteer.

How to Make a Display of Gazetteers

1. Make sure every gazetteer entry has a title.
The title should name the country.

2. Organize all the gazetteer entries alphabetically.
Look at the title of each entry. Put the gazetteer entries in alphabetical order by country.

3. Number the pages.
Add the page number for each page.

4. Prepare a table of contents.
Look at the table of contents in other books. Now make one for your book.

5. Make a cover.
Talk with your classmates about what you all want on the cover. Choose a picture that will tell what the book is about. Then make your cover.

6. Now bind the pages together.
You can staple the pages together. Or you can punch holes on the left side and tie the pages together with yarn.

Glossary

carnivals – celebrations where people feast, hold parades, and dress in costume

challenges – difficulties to be overcome

contribute – to give toward a common purpose

culture – the traditions, language, dress, ceremonies, and other ways of life that a group of people share

discrimination – unfair treatment of people because of their race, sex, or religion

economy – a system of making, managing, and spending money

immigrate – to move to a new country to live

poverty – the state of being poor

reggae – a form of popular music that developed in Jamaica

taxes – money people must pay to the government

unemployment – the state of not having a job

Index